The Accidental Poet

The Poems of Ross Dix-Peek

Eloquent Books

Biographical Details

Ross Dix-Peek was born in Salisbury, Rhodesia (now Harare, Zimbabwe) in July 1970, and subsequently grew up and was educated in South Africa,matriculating at the Hill College, in Port Elizabeth. A fifth-generation Southern African (of British, Irish and Dutch descent), he now resides in Swords, Dublin, Ireland. He came late to poetry (being 38 years-of-age when he began writing poems), and his other interests include Sport, History and Military History, the English Language and Writing.

Contents

Preface

This book is aptly titled *The Accidental Poet* because that is how it all began for me. I was thirty-eight years old when, in a moment of whimsy, I decided to write my first poem. I was rather surprised at the outcome. . . It seemed to be okay, at least passable for a poem. Poetry was never a passion, but once I penned my first poem I realised that I loved writing poetry and continued to do so. Metaphorically, I had stumbled on the world of poetry and found a way to express myself, as well as indulge my love affair for the English language. It is all neatly ensconced in a single package. However, these poems are probably not to everybody's liking. They encapsulate my views and eccentricities; my world-view or "Weltanschauung", and can be a bit dark at times. But, I do have one word of advice for any budding poet; that is rejection is a part of life. You are very likely to be exposed to it, just as I have been. But, whatever you do, never ever give up!

Most importantly of all, I wish to dedicate my book to my late father and sister, Errol Dix-Peek, and Meryl Grebe, whomI miss each and every day, and without the love, patience, under-standing, kind words and unfailing support of my beloved wife, Deanna, my dearest mother, Felicity, and my two wonderful sib-lings, Shelly and Harland, I would never have had the strength nor the determination to go ahead and attempt to get my book published. I also wish to thank Strategic Books (including Elo-quent Books), and all concerned, for giving me that chance! .

Ross Dix-Peek
Swords, Dublin
Republic of Ireland
11 March 2010

The Accidental Poet

The Poems of Ross Dix-Peek

Mom!

Mom, I see you sitting in your chair,
Your face serene, your grey hair fair,
My mind strips away the years,
The countless times you wiped my tears

Never failing, always there for me,
But this I so often did not see,
I owe so very, very much to you,
Times of trouble, you got me through

A caring and kind word there,
Always a nurturing smile to spare,
Forever a guiding light,
Constant and unending bright

Solace from life's storm,
Always loving and true to form,
You saw things I could never see,
But, you were always there to warn me

And even when I was patently wrong,
Your kind words a soothing song,
Your quiet wisdom I always admired,
Sound advice in life sired

And now, as the years slowly fade,
As soft memories silently parade,
There is something you need to know,
Mom, I will always love you so!

(Dedicated to my beloved mother, Felicity Dix-Peek)

Ross Dix-Peek

A Very Brief History of the World

It all began with the Big Bang,
With Genesis the birth pang,
Then came the Dinosaur,
And all that went before

With evolution came man,
When the world's woes began,
With the Euphrates civilisation,
And the seed of city state and nation

Then Ancient Egypt to the fore,
With Hieroglyphics came writing and more,
The great pyramids arose,
And the pharaohs in mighty pose

Across the divide the ancient Greek,
Also an empire sought to seek,
With them came Democracy,
Education and philosophy

With the demise of Alexander
Came Rome and later Caesar,
Masters of war and engineering,
Built a vast Empire most searing

Followed by Byzantium and the Hun,
And too the rise of fervid Islam,
And thus the crusades, and the armoured Knight,
Who with long lance sought feudal might

The world in a precarious state,
That for many years would not abate,
Alas, came Genghis Khan and his dreadful horde,
Brought horrid death with bow and crimson sword

Later Machiavelli, the De Medici's and the Pope
All consummate masters of the long rope,
While in Germany, his anger incandescent and raw,
Martin Luther nailed his 95 demands to a church door

And then gone was the Dark Ages,
Written woeful in history's pages,
Across the ocean sailed an Italian upon the stage,
Columbus was his name, and the dawn of a new age

While arise king Henry with bloodlust to sate,
Had a fevered penchant, a penchant to decapitate,
Came the British Empire, bathed the world in red,
Gave both good and bad, lambent hope and horrid dread

And in the recesses, a war most remote,
Between the colonists and the redcoat,
Gave rise to a new empire, a sleeping giant,
A great colossus, and not always compliant

In the interim, the French revolution,
With war and blood in great profusion,
Napoleon in pomp and Imperial stride,
At Waterloo, Wellington held back the tide

Midst all, the Industrial Revolution was apace,
England abuzz and afoot to win the race,
But in the maelstrom mother and child lost,
Great commercial gain, but, at what cost?

Later came dreadful conflagration and fire,
Two world wars, mad man's most hateful ire,
And yet, still man does not learn,
For money and power eternal does he yearn

And all the while the world marched on,
Came mini-skirts, the Beatles and Vietnam,
And then a new millennium and perhaps new hope,
But 9/11 and the recession meant man was still a dope

And yet, ever is man in war mired,
In Iraq and Afghanistan the troops so very tired,
Still the world's pain belaboured borne,
And what of the future? great bounty or hope forlorn?

Ireland on a Sunny Day!

A Glorious Burst of
Golden Sun,
upon a great "canvas" rendered!
Heaven's warmth sent!
The sky, a majestic blue!
A vast mantle of joy,
The streets vibrant and alive,
People a-hustle and a-bustle,
Milling to and fro,
Excitable chatter,
The Irish tongue a-wag,
Cars, bicycles, motorcycles
and big yellow buses,
The day a rich tapestry of colour,
Apparel and clothing of every hue,
Verdant, luxuriant grass,
Beneath tall towering trees,
A million shades of green,
The flowers a veritable artist's palette,
White, Yellow, Blue, and Red,
The birds infused with life's joy,
Their magnificent song
a most heavenly and divine choir,
Its sweet dulcet tones
cosseting happy, laughing
children at play,
while mottled Butterflies float
lazily upon the soft breeze,
All is so very alive!
Ireland is alive!
But, Alas, a sad portent,
For in the distance,
A most dark, pregnant sky!

What the Hell is Love?

What the Hell is Love?
Is it a blessing from above?
Could it be a feeling most intense?
Or just plain old common-sense?

Perhaps merely an illusion?
Or just mental confusion?
Is it really tingles all over?
Or a field of verdant clover?

Does it make one happy and glow?
Is it just something you know?
Could it be a loyal or funny friend?
Who with one will journey to life's end

May it possibly be a like mind?
Someone intelligent and kind?
Or is it all that and so much more?
A great gilded world yet to explore

The answer I surely do not know,
But I will tell you this, and so,
If it were not for love, most empty the world would be,
For only in your eyes can I find happiness, joy and glee!

The Painting

The painting hangs limp upon the wall,
From its deepest recesses a faint call,
Quiet echoes of a distant dawn,
Fresh brushstrokes upon a canvas drawn

Undulating hills and a valley green,
Verdant pasture a bright sheen,
A glorious glow of orange light
Upon the scene pulses most bright

In my heart a fiery warmth met,
Ever-more emotion yet,
And in a thrumming heart-beat,
Soul and image dare to meet

The painting calls in muted delight,
Borne aloft in ethereal flight,
And in a blessed moment most kissed,
Only my soul, colour and canvas exist

My Pal, Stewart!

My pal Stewart was one of a kind,
The type you'd go far to find,
Always a hearty hello and a rampant smile,
Always willing to go the extra mile

I still remember the soft echoes of his voice,
A man among men, a Rolls-Royce,
He stood well over six-foot tall,
Yet forever gentle with everything and all

Oh, Stewie was a damn funny guy,
Always a mischievous sparkle in the eye,
And with an apt turn of phrase and wit,
He would always have us in a laughing fit

There were two passions in his life,
One was cricket, the other his dear wife,
A skilled and fantastic umpire was he,
Stewart was really something to see

Thus he was always in the sun a lot,
And in Africa it's always so very hot,
Saw a doctor about a pesky mole one day,
And learnt he had cancer that way

Yet he never moaned nor complained,
Never felt sorry for himself nor feigned,
And although he battled ever most bold,
Dire death was ultimately to take hold

Our beloved Stewie was with us no more,
My battered, broken heart rattled to the core,
And although he's been gone for quite a while,
I will always remember my dear pal, and his sunny smile!

(In tribute to my beloved friend, Stewart Deenik, who sadly succumbed to cancer on the 25 August 2007...He will forever live on in my heart!)

This Person Called Me!

I am merely me,
The only person I can be,
Mortality my only shawl,
With glaring faults and all

Tried to please all the time,
Just a pathetic pantomime,
Hostage to unfounded fears,
Wasted so many years

To many a tune I used to sing,
Merely a puppet on a string,
And the more I duly tried,
The more my very soul died

At last it dawned on me,
In a moment of sheer clarity,
That the only person I could ever be,
Was this person called me!

A Murder in Padua, 1395 AD

There lived in the foothills of Padua,
A most solitary monk named Capua,
Who with great genius and creativity
Was known to solve nearly every mystery

In 1395, a murder most foul,
Took place in a monastery's inner bowel,
A monk had, it seemed, been slain,
But what had caused his deathly bane?

So pondered Capua as he hurried away,
To journey to the scene of dark dismay,
Received with suspicion and yet respect,
He soon began to most sedulous detect

He scoured the inner sanctum most awake,
Searching for any clue that could the mystery break,
But none did perchance come to the fore,
Perhaps hidden everlasting and forevermore

But not discouraged was this monk, not him,
He would find the killer with vigour and vim,
Capua then began in earnest to study
The poor monk's dead and lifeless body

Around the man's mouth a toxin he espied,
The feint trace of Strychnine, Death's Bride,
His avails then led him to the murdered monks room,
Where still permeated a sad pall of gloom

The monk had apparently hung himself,
But this was not surely the truth in itself,
For astride the wooden chair and in the dusty dirt,
Capua could see three sets of footprints, most alert

There were also two strands of cloth to be seen,
One the same and one of a different colour and sheen,
But the dead monk had but cloaks of one colour, Brown,
Pondered Capua most intense, what had gone down?

In addition, slight specks of white stuff,
Flour, he deduced and then wiped on his cuff,
And then to the kitchen and larder next,
He was now sure the suicide was a mere pretext

A few hours of detection and he was ready
To pronounce the true cause, his voice steady,
All he gathered most anxious before him,
Nervously awaiting the wise monk's requiem

No, this was not suicide, he frankly said,
But a murder most vile put to bed,
The deceased monk had discovered a secret vice,
For which he was to pay the ultimate price

The kitchen staff and others too,
Were selling stolen produce without its due,
Upon this murky trade had the dead man stumbled,
And thus into the deep bowels of death tumbled

It seems he was bribing them, a most silly thing to do,
And the sordid idea of a murder soon began to brew,
The evil-doers then concocted their malicious plan,
And quietened the monk before his mouth ran,

They poisoned him first and then feigned suicide,
And about an encroaching madness lied,
But, they had not reckoned with the genius from Padua,
The Argus-eyed sleuth, a monk named Capua!

The Loser!

They called him a loser,
Was also a bit of a boozer,
Not the most responsible chap,
Had quite a criminal rap

Divorced twice with kids,
His life constantly on the skids,
Most thought him less than lice,
Addicted to almost every vice

But then one day without much ado or fuss
He saved a little girl from being hit by a bus,
Not much of him left to scrape off the street,
But the little girl survived, how sweet

A quaint little dilemma now you see,
Indeed yet another societal mystery,
Yes, he was a loser once, and how,
But what, might we ask, was he now?

Ross Dix-Peek

Teenage Pregnancy!

Anxious and worried smile,
The awful taste of rising bile,
What will my dad say?
Torrid anger or abject dismay?

Mom's innocent little girl,
Her bright button and dear pearl,
Dreams forever shattered and gone,
Where once only the soft sun shone

But, do I want this child?
Emotions rampant and so wild!
Ever burgeoning evidence,
Prying eyes most intense,

Whatever shall I do?
This world so dark and very blue,
Fingers pointed in my direction,
Naught but pain and introspection

And what of the child's dad?
Whatever is to be had?
Not a woman, just a little girl,
In Life's spiralling swirl

Slut, I hear them all say,
Tears swelling each and every day,
Sardonic titters here and there,
Caustic jibes fill the air

But, No, I will not succumb,
If need be, I will be a Mum,
Come what ever will and may,
I shall carry my babe, and the day!

To at last hold my dear soft bundle,
And through life's travails to trundle,
Together joyous we both will be,
Mother and child in life's journey!

Poor Mabel!

Poor old Mabel,
Sedulous and able,
With bucket,mop and broom,
She cleans every room,
For 30 years she's toiled,
Never from hard work recoiled,
Never a peep nor complaint,
Always shown noble restraint,
But to the company hard times came,
All knew it would never be the same,
Oh, what now, they all said,
Arms aloft and all in dread,
Someone's head had to be chopped,
Someone's job had to be dropped,
And surprise, surprise,
Midst the assurances and lies,
Between her and the lazy CEO
It was poor Mabel that had to go!

An African Sun!

Great copper orb cast on high,
Fierce and fiery delight in a vast blue sky,
A burning, billowing furnace open drawn,
Upon an enigmatic, ancient African dawn,

A Great spurt of orange coloured hue
explodes most profuse upon a regal view,
To infuse life most intense and fine,
The vast African veld so divine,

Tall brown elephant grass burned and dry
Bows before a most marvellous majestic sky,
As the denizens of the dark bush begin to stir,
And scurry back and forth in excited whirr,

All under a guiding and most noble hand,
A great gilded effusion upon the land,
To bestow its ancient and bounteous reward,
Upon its dear children, amazed and awed,

And when comes the dark, inky night,
And is lost upon the eye a most revered sight,
All wait for foul nocturne to be undone,
And yet again to see the gold-plated Sun!

Meet the Dawn!

The ink-black night retreats,
Comes the first blush of dawn,
Its long luminous fingers unravel
night's dense dark blanket

The soft kiss of silken light falls upon
Hope's waiting lips,
Night's insecurities and anguish begin
Slowly to vanish 'midst a most brilliant and fulgent embrace

Welcome Day advances lazy,
Almost surreptitiously, yet inexorably,
to vanquish the vast dark juggernaut,
as sweet joy does then sing unrestrained, unbridled

A euphonious melody, a most wondrous and exultant
    symphony,
While the last slivers of darkness genuflect forlorn and
    submissive
before the great "Illume",
Kneeling to a greater, unrelenting force

And then is gone dire darkness,
And before my very eyes
do the steel bars of Night's awful "cage", wither and wilt,
and at last, spent, does succumb to the great bliss that is the
    Sweet Dawn's Kiss!

The Soldier

From the very dawn of time
They've left their homes with dreams fine,
Ready for battle and hearts ablaze
Swords unsheathed for hellfire days,
Their noble breasts to the fore

But soon the hell of war
Does destroy the vital core,
Gone is the eager smile
And the mere thought of battle most vile
Frayed nerves, tender and raw

The awful days proceed unending
Many a dear friend's soul ascending,
The indelible stain of young men's blood
Sacrificed to the gods of war in a ceaseless flood,
Reason has fled, no-where to be seen

All that is left is benumbing dread and fear,
And the Thousand-Yard Stare,
Each day a quest for survival
Each day but to Kill, Kill, Kill!
Death's stalking shadow ever-present and near

And yet, Wars beating drum still beats aloud
A dark, morbid and fitful cloud,
To the benumbed soldier, all is in vain
As life's fancy begins ever to wane,
The awful cries of the vanquished, the only sound

And when the crimson sword is again sheathed
And the comfort of home to the soldier bequeathed,
All that remains is the silent, haunting night
Unwanted memories and a fevered mind in fright,
His shackled soul never to be freed!

21

Ross Dix-Peek

It is only the Grim Reaper and death's ardent ring
That peace to the anguished warrior can bring,
It is only the shedding of mortal anger and regret
That shall his martial soul cause to forget,
And then, at last content, to rise on-high upon an angel's wing!

The Cashier

Each day a constant blur,
Not an ember of hope astir,
Silent shadows slither slowly by,
Apt to deceive the waiting eye

Now and again a glance,
Now and again a look askance,
Possibly a word or two,
The world a big blanket of blue

Underpaid and not appreciated,
Dear dreams withered and abated,
A mere robot in suspended motion,
Life now nothing more than mere notion

The eyes dead and benumb,
The clock on the wall a slaving drum,
Minutes and hours all the same,
A slow, strangled death by any other name

But at last ceases eternity,
And gone is vile misery,
Perhaps, now a new day and dawn,
But sadly, naught but hope forlorn!

Lost At Sea!

Solitary and stark stands the memorial,
A granite-grey testimonial
To Old King Neptune's sons and daughters,
Asleep silent beneath the cold waters,
Now in death's repose, brothers and sisters all
Beneath the vast watery shawl,
The white-crested waves do them loving adorn,
Poseidon's royal crown upon the great ocean borne,
The most noble and exalted deep
their immortal lair and keep,
And now and forever-again
To stand dear sentinel over them,
Their souls never again to know foul fear,
Never again to shed an earthly and torrid tear,
Their worldly woes forever ceased,
At last to know the gentle kiss of eternal peace,
And now beneath the briny coffin shroud,
Their sweet serenity is at last avowed!

Neptune's Call

In the distance a Royal chariot borne most prolific and proud,
Sails serene upon mother wind, the soft snowy spray
of a great wallowing wave, while atop and aloft rides Noble
    Neptune,
his clarion cry and call mingles most melodious
with the sweet murmur of the ocean,
this vast sweeping sheet of glassy sea green
swaying like a sedulous metronome against
the torrid tide of time, upon the wind and aether
can be heard the distant dulcet tones and
sweet strains of a Mermaid's sensual song,
and at last, this ample bounty of bedazzling beauty,
this great juggernaut of the distant deep,
this rhythmical and gallant guardian of mortal man,
tumbles most savage and yet serene,
to wash wet upon the soft sand of a salient shore,
the skies riven and rent asunder by Poseidon's mighty roar!

The Boxer

The boxer stands with his gloves at the ready
His gait sure and steady
His eyes aware and to the fore
His mind on the bout and nothing more

But deep within, and on his face written
Are the many scars of a life hard-bitten
And while never shy of a hard-fought fight
There is no longer within the feeling of delight

His face has too often been made to pay
By an opponent far better on the day,
And though within beats the heart of a lion
His poor pummelled flesh has given up tryin'

And while a fighter to the very core
Just the smell of gloves now he does abhor,
Yet, still he stands, eyes puffed and blood galore
Still ready to wage the pugilist's war

As blow after blow upon his battered head does fall,
He knows but only one way, and that is the brawl,
And even though his broken body has since given in,
The spirit of the fighter knows no such thing!

The Duel

The lords did not on some point agree,
An indignant slight perceived, you see,
And so, in some secluded dale,
To a duel they did then avail

With the coming of the dawn,
And with guns anxious drawn,
They began their nervous steps apace,
All in a foolish bid to save face

It mattered not now who was to blame,
As they turned and took hurried aim,
And soon was the air rent asunder
In a hail of smoke and booming thunder,

One bullet flew to rattle a bird in a tree,
The other also amiss by some great degree,
And then, with honour appeased and rage at bay,
The two lords, hand in arm, did saunter away!

The Fisherman's Moon

The dark docile waters glimmer, shimmer and dance
in the milky moonlight glow of a warm, sultry night,
fishing rods at the ready and languid lines immersed,
The ink-black night punctuated
by the quiet whispers of eager, expectant
anglers, eagle-eyed and intent upon
the glassy, spangled surface of a fisherman's delight,
a sip of cold coffee or Satan's Brew
and the night hangs heavy, ready and most pregnant,
beneath the waters scurry scaled prey,
alert yet ever-desirous
of the nagging need of their big bulbous bellies,
The scene set midst the glowing, incandescent
embers of a crackling fire, and as the
sands of time slowly ebb, mere minutes
and then hours, who will possess the
staying power, the sharp, steely resolve,
the fisherman's weary eyelids hang heavy with
each passing moment, the attentive arms of Morpheus await,
but wait! A faint nagging nibble, and again!
The line and the reel suddenly agog, awhizz
and awhirl, the great game afoot, the anglers'
taut and ready, their eager eyes splendidly a-sparkle with
avid anticipation in the ghostly light of a pale pallid
moon, proud predator and poor prey pulsating to
the march of an atavistic, primordial drum, the hunter
and the hunted, sweet life, stark death, the quiet
refrains of an amphibious battle borne aloft
upon the fleeting, fitful winds of a dark soulful night,
and in the dismal dreary depths of a watery tomb,
the poor, valiant silver scaled foe
begins to wearily wane before the solid and steady
resolve of the hunter's will…
to finally flop and flounder upon a waiting riverbank,

its very life-force spent, and at a perilous and parlous end it
    seems,
above, the silent, shadowy blur of a grasping hand…
but the high Heavens' have smiled,
the great Gods' merciful, for this intrepid finned foe
is soon unleashed to again grace the murky depths
of its vast, watery domain,
a doughty denizen of the dear deep,
The fisherman's fevered brow and
fiery eyes alight,
The great and honourable contest is done,
and Victory is indeed sweet!

*(Written in tribute to my dear departed father, Errol Dix-Peek,
a most avid and skilful angler)*

Ross Dix-Peek

Henry Ford Had an Idea!

Henry Ford had an idea so very bright
To build a little car, affordable, rugged and light,
And, so was born the old "Tin Lizzie",
That veritable man-made prodigy,

Built in droves upon a factory line
To Mr Ford's good and able design,
And soon was his little joy and pride
Shipped to all, far and wide

From America to Africa,
From Eurasia to Australia,
Was to be seen the little car, always in "black",
On roads fair, or off the beaten track

To businessmen and farmers all,
"Tin Lizzie" did them always enthral,
Never a problem nor grey day,
The little marvel always led the way

Now gone, and no more,
Just a dear memory, folklore,
Sadly, today's cars merely a "thing"
Just built to entice, all about the "Bling"!

*(A tribute to Henry Ford and his 1908 Ford T, the famous "Tin
Lizzie")*

I Chanced Upon a Time

I chanced upon a time,
Most noble and divine,
Where war was no more,
And death a thing of lore

I walked through golden fields,
Where great bounty yields,
And felt the warmth of an undying Sun,
Life's gentle thread never undone

The only sound, peace,
An enveloping gilded fleece,
Where greed and avarice abstain,
And hunger is a fallow field lain

Where equality is not just a word,
And kings and queens but absurd,
Where men and women are born free,
And so remain for eternity

Where only life's nectar avails,
And suffering no longer prevails,
Where hardship is laid to bed,
And gone is awful dread

Where man's needs genuflect before his will,
And life is serene and most beautiful,
But Alas! It would but seem,
I awoke to find but a dream!

The Wife-Beater

He was always happy and friendly,
So very handsome, cool and trendy,
Always witty, charming and funny,
And never failed to take home the money

But behind closed doors, a Demon incarnate,
Ruled relentless over a woman's helpless fate,
His feelings paramount, his word set in stone,
No life had she, it belonged to him alone

Never could she criticise nor scoffer,
Never a word to the contrary proffer,
The beatings brutal and intense,
Hidden from the world, a most silent fence

To her fate was she resigned,
A fragile Angel and the Devil aligned,
Hid her bruises from prying eyes,
A constant stream of excuses and lies

Wanted to leave him, but couldn't you see,
For no support and skills had she,
But, trapped in his cage, a never-ending vice,
Nothing she did would ever suffice

Once, the police knocked upon her door,
Heard the commotion and the uproar,
But, the wife-beater explained all away,
And the only thing she could do, was pray

For her dear children she stayed,
Her fear and emotion briefly allayed,
In sheer desperation again to try,
But only sad misery did the future espy

Alas, they found her body one misty morn,
Lying most still, alone and forlorn,
So different, could have been her fate,
But, All far too little, far too late!

*(Dedicated to all woman who suffer the silent Hell of an
abusive boyfriend or husband)*

Ross Dix-Peek

Luminous Thoughts

With electric clarity they pierce my mind,
Luminous thoughts that serve to bind,
The ghostly thread of a pale dawn,
Across a sprawling sky drawn

To alight most noble upon the mind's page,
The soft, silken words of a mysterious age,
Wherein, mute echoes serve to resound,
And silent refrains ably abound

A great kaleidoscopic mind's eye,
The fleeting glimpse of an amorphous butterfly,
That most gentle and high aloft
Descends upon a white cloud serene and soft

A vivid rainbow caught in a billowing sail,
Abstract strands visible and yet pale,
Beleaguered thought in a fevered embrace,
At last to find peace in a heavenly place!

"Hollywood Vows" (Satirical Poem)

I promise never to love you,
Nor ever to hold you,
If this so-called marriage lasts but a week
Believe me, that shall be quite a feat,
I promise never to cherish you
And always to be untrue,
For you I shall not care,
For you I cannot bear
Hate and disdain is all I can offer,
And vile vanity all I can proffer,
I promise only greed and mammon to adore,
And for you I shall only but abhor,
And when life is good and fair
I shall then still be there,
But when I distant clouds do see
Then do I thee promise to flee,
I promise only to remain for life's sweet "honey"
And to fleece you of all your money,
And when your hair and looks do fade
So then shall I thee farewell bade,
I promise to often make you cry
And your sad tears never to dry,
And if reward my way could come
I promise to murder you, and then some,
I promise to drive you to suicide
And for you never to provide,
When your figure rotund does become
Then shall I for the fair hills run,
I promise to make your days so very "blue"
And to make our dear children hate you too,
I promise never to by your side lay
Unless you remunerate me for time spent, and the day,
Comfort you shall never know,
And anguish shall be your only shadow,

Ross Dix-Peek

Worriment and distress shall also your companions be,
And I promise, me you shall hardly ever see
So, let's get this damn farce over with, why don't we!

(This is merely satire and my opinion of Hollywood marriages)

Rwandan Elegy

The foul stench of burning flesh permeates the air,
Rotten, putrefying bodies lie in the baking sun,
Bright crimson death everywhere,
Frightened masses on the run

Wide-eyed terror on the prowl,
Africa rent asunder,
Can be seen death's fervid scowl,
Sheer madness in Rwanda

Frenzied killing unabated,
A fevered orgy of blood,
Hate and bloodlust not sated,
A vile and incessant flood

Machete's a-glint in the firelight,
Dark night knows no end,
Rampant death beneath stars bright,
The victims' souls ascend

Sculpted in lifeless repose,
Torn bodies and silent screams,
The legion of dead in abject throes,
Life now naught but the residue of dreams

And, where must be asked, was the World
When they were needed the most?
Why were their actions not most bold?
Why was saving lives not foremost?

And today, the land lies sullied in shame,
The rabid killers remain unbowed,
The dark pall of hate still silently aflame,
And beyond, a menacing cloud

Ross Dix-Peek

But perhaps from the ashes of the dead,
Rwanda can rise once more,
To assuage the blood, terror and dread,
And embrace peace forevermore!

I Will Always Love You!

I know what I know,
It's always been so,
I say what I say,
Until my dying day,
Uncompromising and to the fore,
That's just me to the very core,
Put my foot in it all the time,
Sometimes surreal, sometimes sublime,
Mouth's a little too slick,
And often far too quick,
Don't think before I speak,
And you can't call me meek,
Not always romantic am I,
Not always understanding when you cry,
But believe me, I know this I do,
Yep, I will always, always love you!

The Land of My Heart, Rhodesia!

Rhodesia, land of my heart,
Oh, wondrous and rugged jewel,
Whence my soul shall never part,
And forever love most purposeful

Most majestic nation of yesteryear,
And Pride of Africa indeed,
Forever ensconced in memory most fair,
Oh country of noble breed

For many you shall never die,
Always to flourish anew,
Your vast cerulean sky
A beloved imprint most true

Bulawayo, Kariba, the Great Zambezi,
Their noble names a melodious song,
The Matopos, Gwelo, Umtali and Salisbury,
Will in memory forever live on

And, when I do leave this mortal coil behind,
And most pale do lie in deathly leisure,
Upon my lifeless heart they shall find
Only one word, "Rhodesia"!

*(This poem has nothing to do with politics, it is merely a
heartfelt tribute to the land of my birth...Rhodesia!)*

The Springbok

The Springbok runs supreme,
Fleet-footed and light
Fast, lithe and lean,
An awe-inspiring sight,
With noble ingenuity
He weaves in and out,
Sublime sinuosity,
The defence in rout,
To place the oval ball
Behind the hallowed line
"Green and Gold" the call,
All so divine,
while on a patch of grass,
Plays a little boy,
Throws a well-timed pass,
His heart awash with joy,
And dreams of that day,
When he too in "Green and Gold"
Will join the mighty fray
Steadfast and most bold,
At last to take his worthy place
Among these revered men,
To pit his wiles and grace,
Against the best, again and again
Ah, Those dear old enemies,
Across the rugby divide,
The British Lions, All Blacks and Wallabies
The prize, national pride,
But, he wishes most of all
With resolve, grit and pluck,
To stand, most proud and tall,
A mighty "Springbok"

Ross Dix-Peek

The White African

Over the great ocean seas
My ancestors did choose to flee
Europe's rumblings and poverty,
And to "Darkest Africa" journey

It was many, many years past,
When Queen Vic' was still at the mast
When my forebears resolute did come
To live 'neath the great African sun

Since has Mother Africa suckled our young
To us her lullaby's and sweet songs sung
And all this time 'neath her fiery mantle
Did my people in Africa live, toil and battle

Africa is not for the mild and the meek
It is no place at all for the feeble and the weak,
And the days oft be savage and so very long
Yes, it is only for the brave and the very strong

Many generations did pass, and many years shorn
Before I too upon African soil was born,
Like my fathers' before, a White African
Created and cast 'neath her scorching sun

And although I have since her rugged shores left
My soul to Mother Africa's bosom will forever be cleft,
And though I may miss the tight embrace of an African sun
It matters not, for I will forever be a White African!

We Are All Somebody!

We are all somebody, telling and real,
No matter how insignificant we may feel,
Each its own magical masterpiece,
Given this blessing, life's lease,
Every person important in some special way,
To all, a divine birthright to have our say,
Indeed, all so very unique,
Different dreams and desires we seek,
Varying talents, strengths and abilities,
Each life its own sanctuary,
Every soul a fertile field,
Dependent on us as to what we yield,
None better than the rest,
Each life its own true test,
Upon a temporal anvil, a life wrought,
Some easy, but some dear bought,
Trials and tribulations upon us all,
To walk, stumble and fall,
Not a single life cheap,
Each with gilded scythe to reap,
Every soul a speck of sable sand,
Every life a delicate, frail and fragile strand,
Sacred existence under a bronzed Sun
Whimsically welded together as one,
Upon this celestial orb we spin,
Fused and fastened in mortal unison!

Boys Flinging Mud-Pies!

My mind harks back to another day,
To Africa and a shallow riverbed,
Three young boys at play,
Wet mud all about and overhead

We're playing our favourite game,
The "Art" of flinging mud-pies,
Hiding, and taking careful aim,
Shrill laughter fills the skies

The "enemy" clearly in sight,
Mud "loaded" on the end of a stick,
The Sun so very warm and bright,
And then, "Bombs Away" with a deft flick

"Got Him" I yell with sheer glee,
But not long is it before
A thick dollop of wet clingy mud strikes me,
"Ah, damn" I shout with a happy roar

What fun, all day we would scurry
To and fro in that old riverbed,
In a paroxysm of playful flurry,
As the Sun slowly waned overhead

All muddied and gooey,
And very dirty we were,
Truly, it was ecstasy,
The day just one big happy blur

And then, unfortunately, the time would come
And we would have to go,
Always made us feel a bit glum,
Trudged back home so very slow

And as we left that old riverbed,
I would always look back,
And still it lives in my mind, never dead,
A well-worn memory, a mental bivouac!

Death's Chugging Bus

Ah, Sir, you think you're cool,
But like all of us, really just a fool,
Think you know it all,
Well, you're in for quite a fall,

King or pauper it's all the same,
We're all just playing the guessing game,
Living this most tantalising lie,
Really, all just waiting to die,

All just biding our time,
Waiting for that solitary chime,
When to knock upon death's door,
And to be no more

Waiting for death's chugging bus to come along,
So, why all the damn fuss, why the silly song?
You know, it really matters not,
No, not a single, single jot,

Unto each his own illusion,
Unto each his own delusion,
It matters not who you are, or what you say,
All that's important is this dear day!

Here Comes the Rain!

Soft patter upon my window,
Above, clouds most grey,
The sound of sweet rain a-flow,
Bejewelled ribbons at play,

Cascading petals of sweet reprieve,
Fall on parched soil,
Ever -eager to receive,
Thus to end the day's toil

And when the rain has fled,
And in the distance lost,
A new "Eden" bred,
Heaven and Earth crossed

A bedazzling dash of colour,
Of every shade and hue,
What divine splendour,
As all begins anew

And with the new start,
A Joyous melody and song,
Perhaps, a change-of-heart,
And to embrace life, most strong!

Ross Dix-Peek

Mother Africa!

Africa beats a proud tattoo upon my heart,
Its ancient glory my heritage,
Its great azure sky my eternal solace,
Born to "Mother Africa",
I cling to her bosom,
Her loving child forevermore,
Although wild, savage and unrelenting,
Beneath the majestic copper sun,
She remains my beloved "home",
Her sunburnt realm my souls abode,
Never to relinquish her sweet hold,
And across the great ocean divide
I still long for her,
To feel her assured warmth
upon my brow,
Her loving rays upon my face,
To again immerse myself
in her great splendour,
And to tread underfoot her most ancient soil,
To once more behold her natural wonders,
Her vast and glorious majesty,
And although her dear soul
Lies wracked by fitful convulsions,
Of poverty, terror and abject horror ,
Her beloved children most restless,
Africa will again rise, rise she will,
A veritable Goddess,
To again stand bestride the world,
In candescent Glory,
Finally to take her rightful place
Amidst history's splendid pantheon,
Oh Mother Africa, I do thee adore!

Never Give Up!

When all is so bleak
And the mind and body so very weak
When life's travails
Your being assails
Never Give Up!

When to live is but strife
In this fitful endeavour called life
When to be, brings only anguish and pain
And the mind no-longer seems at all sane
Never Give Up!

When your poor bleeding heart so ails
And there be no winds of fortune in your sails
When each day brings but only misery and strife
In this great quagmire called Life
Never Give Up!

When great dark storms your flimsy ship do batter
And your heartfelt dreams do shatter
When distress your aching heart does rend
And the Gods no providence do send
Never Give Up!

When your only bedfellow be but misfortune
And trouble your only ken
When stygian darkness and endless night
Dear and eternal hope put to flight
Never Give Up!

For I promise you my Dear Friend
There will come but an end
To all your grief and sorrow
And in time, hope bright and effulgent light will greet your
    Tomorrow
So Never Give Up!

Ross Dix-Peek

The Real Weapons of Mass Destruction!

Arms aloft and in the air
The politicians shout, "Beware!"
Of the "Weapons of Mass Destruction",
Again it is mere "Spin"

For the real worry is not the WMD's,
Bin Laden, Al Qaeda, or the Iraqis
It is indeed far closer to home
That the threat does unbridled roam

These pernicious maladies
Afflict us all, and our dear families
And indeed take a far greater toll
Than an imagined nuclear bomb in some hell-hole

And yet very few are alarmed,
Hardly anybody "up in arms",
And no politician or anyone,
Does this vile malaise shun

For, far more dangerous than some despot's vitriol
Are the "terrible twins", cigarettes and alcohol,
So many more lives thus destroyed and devastated
Than some little lunatic aggravated

And still these "terrible twins" do us "ill",
Still our children and loved one's kill
And yet, no warnings, no uproar,
No protestations galore!

Why is that so?
But the answer we already know,
For , in the "corridors of power"
"Money" and "Greed" does the conscience devour

So when you next chance upon a "drunk"
Or see a "smoker" in a coffin sunk,
Then perhaps may you see
Where the "Real Weapons of Mass Detruction" be!

The Castle

Through ages past have ye stood sentinel and proud
And ne'er by the enemy's sword been cowed
Your great walls ever steadfast and resolute
And even did the onslaught of time put to boot

Ah, ye great big monster of stone, if only you could talk
And with us through the pages of history walk
What could you tell us of ages gone by
Of the horrors perpetrated within and why?

Would your walls again with awful cries resonate
Of the vanquished and the unfortunate
Would the sky above and this verdant view
Turn to a dark pall of bloody hue

Would thy be able to hold back the souls of the tortured
That within your deep dark dungeons their lives forfeited
And upon your cold grey slabs of stone did lie
Before the vultures the cold flesh from their very bones did
    pry

No, O' Great Castle I think not I your secrets want to know
And I'm sure you too do not your vile memories wish to show
It be best rather if you and I your ghastly past do forget
And instead upon a far better future our dreams and hopes do
    set!

The Door

I may just but be a door
But I am indeed far more
I am the gateway to many worlds
The timeless observer of Life's many folds
Janus-faced, I see all before

You cannot hide from my all-seeing eyes
Your inner-most secrets you cannot disguise
I am always privy to your world
And your dearest dreams and desires all-told
And I see all life's truths and lies

Whether gilded or shoddy
I am the guardian of man's folly
The eternal keeper of secrets and woes
It is I who shrouds life's throes
And protects man's realm from sully

So, when your eyes next alight upon my frame
Remember I am far more than my humble name
For it is before my very feet
That two-worlds do meet
For I am the Keeper of the Twain!

Ross Dix-Peek

The Economist

He sits upright and most refined,
Spews forth the litany of a small mind,
Proffers opinions with a smarmy smile,
Empty jargon and a countenance most vile

Thinks he knows all and is quite the best,
And to hell with the "riff-raff" and the rest,
Always in the throes of an epiphany,
Writes books aplenty on the economy

Wears the best, only Armani
And, of course, drives a Ferrari,
Thinks he a prophet and a sage,
A "New-God" in a "New-Age

His pampered face always proud,
His ready mouth always loud,
He really is quite the actor,
Thinks he's the X-Factor

And perforce a lady on each arm,
Smitten with his unctuous charm,
Spends money like there's no tomorrow,
And never has the need to borrow

Wanted on every Talk Show,
Empty words aplenty and quite a-flow,
His face in every paper and magazine,
A Demi-God it seems, really quite obscene

The ignorant masses hang on his every word,
Nothing he says is ever absurd,
Earns a six-figure salary,
And always panders to the gallery

But, when given the noble task,
And this I most humbly ask,
Where was his wise and sagacious intervention,
When needed to pre-empt and forestall the great "Recession"?

(a satirical take on all those so-called financial experts out there who were really quite useless and inept in determining and prohibiting the actual and adverse course of financial events, in other words the "Recession" ...they are really just a "Joke"!)

Ross Dix-Peek

The Stretcher-Bearers

Upon a hill windswept and bleak
Shoulders slumped and most meek,
Came four warriors' worn and weary,
Atop that awful, silent eyrie,
Twixt the four a fallen comrade,
Their tender tears a silent serenade,
The soldier carried from battle's lair,
Great sorrow awaft in the fevered air
Their Eyes most dead and most dull,
Dark burning orbs in a benumbed skull,
And on that hill that very morn,
Did they bury their comrade, of life shorn
And beneath the virgin earth does he now rest
Only a rifle and helmet to mark the very best,
And again, did they melt away,
Back to battle's torrid fray,
In their cluttered minds a warriors' farewell,
And the tolling of yet another bell!

What Does it Take to be Nice?

In truth, what does it take to be nice?
To proffer a complement or two
Even a cursory nod will suffice,
Which for many is long overdue,
And you might just happen to see
Upon proffering a ready smile
A granite frown turn to glee,
And a happy face for a while,
It really does not take much
To light up a person's day,
Nothing but a friendly touch,
And a few good words to say,
You see, naught can withstand
the magic of a friendly "Hello!"
and nor can they misunderstand
a hale and hearty "Cheerio!"
so before you growl and scowl,
and embark upon a diatribe,
or cry most fevered foul,
remember first to prescribe
a wave and a cheerful smile,
a most potent potion for the day,
makes it all so very worthwhile,
as you go upon your way!

Ross Dix-Peek

Aces High!

Silver "dots" ablaze in the bright azure sky
The alarm, "Bandits, 12 O'Clock High!"
"20 plus," shouts the skipper
And to us all, "end that damn chatter!"

Frantically climb to meet the foe
Need altitude, far too low
Can't see anyone
The sun, the damn sun!

Heart a pumpin'
Full of adrenaline
Can see them now,
Going to "bounce us", and how!

"Wingman, stay with me!"
That's me, that's me!
Not long now 'til we meet,
Good old "Spitfire" and the "Messerschmitt"

"Tally-Ho, "and then begins the awful "game"
The bright cerulean sky aflame
Sadly, one of ours gone already
Plummets, an orange flame spewing from his "belly"

"Crikey!", 109 screams past
All so damn fast!
Gone is the "Teutonic Cross"
Too quick, my loss!

Ears abuzz with the squadron chatter
As we all frantically scatter
My eyes anxious the tangled sky search
As beneath me does my "Spitfire" roll and lurch

"Dogfight" now in earnest,
Can't tell ours from the rest
Lost the skipper, can't think
Someone shouts he's "okay, but in the drink"

"Damn!, Damn!"
Not much of a wingman!
Be the butt of all their jokes,
If I ever get back to the blokes

And then, a 109 right in front of me,
My face lights up with glee,
Time to redeem myself
But, slowly, slowly, use stealth

Finger on the trigger
Too late, he's alert and quicker
Frantically dives for the sea
And on his tail, little old me

Engine screaming!
The "old bird" trembling!
Too low, too low!
Can see the foamy white waves just below!

This chap's no novice,
On we plummet to the ocean's surface,
At last, he pulls up,
Thank God, nearly caught me a "scup"

Catch a glimpse of his "cowling"
His crest, aptly a "Knight" scowling!
Closer, ever closer
My "Merlin" a-purr

Now, gently, gently, in my sights
Got him now, by all rights
"Bang", "Crack", "Shudder", I look,
Behind me, oldest trick in the book

"Blighter" jumped me from behind
Another "Emil" 109
"Shell" after damn "shell"
He's sure "ringing the bell"

Engine on fire,
A funeral pyre
Lean back on the "stick"
Climb, climb, and then the "flick!"

Great benevolent sky
Does then me pry
From my burning "pulpit",
Gone forever , my "dear" chariot!

Hit the "brolly",
Feeling pretty damn "sore and sorry"
And then into the cumbered "drink",
Too cold to think!

This "Show" not my best,
Inflate my "Mae West",
My spirits then start to revive,
For am I not still alive!

Look up yonder to the sky
As the "Victors" over me fly
A quick "dip" of their wings
As the "Daimler-Benz" engines sing

And as the cold, icy water my chin gently laps
I then in "salute", raise my hand to the chaps
Although we "Foe" most assuredly may be,
It's good to see, does still live "Chivalry"

But as they slowly disappear
I then do solemn vow and declare
That should I ever again the "Luftwaffe" see,
I that time shall the "Victor" be!

*(A tribute to all the fighter pilots of the Second World War, both
Allied and Axis, amazing men all!)*

*(To "Bounce" in fighter parlance was to attack an enemy
from a superior altitude, and preferably from "out of the
sun"; "My Merlin a-purr" refers to the Spitfire's Rolls Royce
Merlin engine; "The Drink" is the sea; The "Emil" was the
Messerschmitt 109 E (more accurately the BF 109 E); The
"Scup" is an Atlantic fish; "To Ring the Bell" was to get
good results; The "Pulpit" was RAF slang for the cockpit; The
Messerschmitt 109 E3 was powered by the Daimler Benz 6/1A;
To "dip"your wings was to "waggle" the wings to-and-fro in
salute; "Luftwaffe" was the German Air Force)*

Ross Dix-Peek

An Ode to the Autistic Child

I care not for what you wish.
I am a planet unto my own.
To you I am strange.
But, you cannot see my world.

In your world,you are limited.
In mine,I am "King",
Where effulgent stars know no bounds,
And my dreams no limitations.

Think not of my body,
For it does not define who I am.
No, look into my eyes,
For that is the very window to my soul.

To you I am lost,
Needing to be found.
But, while you seek me,
I am at play…

In a world where sunshine is my constant companion,
Where "limitation"is but a word, and joyous freedom a reality,
Where "Peter Pan", "Winnie the Pooh" and "Barney" are my
    dearest friends,
Where I am "Superman", and the world a mere speck in the
    distance.

Instead of searching for me,
Why, my friend, don't you join me?
For it is then, and only then, that you will find me!
For it is then, and only then,… that you will know me!

*(This Poem was written in tribute to the wonderful children
of "Stepping Stones" School, situated near Kilcloon, County
Meath, Ireland)*

Consumerism, Merely Another God!

We don't ask why, we just buy
Seduced by yet another lie,
Told we need,
The subliminal bleed,
Spend, spend, spend
The madness knows no end,
Consumerism, merely another God
And still transfixed, onward we plod,
Desire and possession,
Money the obsession,
Man's maniacal law,
The fiscal flaw,
And meek, do we genuflect
Before the invisible architect,
Told what to wear, and what to eat
What to buy, the ultimate deceit,
And when in debt, spend they say
And like mere robots, we obey,
Not a murmur, Not a whimper,
And still we feed this abject Monster,
And when, I ask, alas and alack,
Will we finally take our lives back!

Dreams!

Dreams, all we have are dear dreams,
Dark clouds with a silver lining,
Feathered beds with gilded seams,
Hopes aloft and ever-pining

Celestial respite
From mortal reality,
A time of newfound delight,
And dear sanity

Ethereal castles in the air,
A world devoid of pain,
A fleeting reprieve from dark despair,
Our souls ever-alive again

New lustre to a waning Sun,
King's finery for a beggar's lair,
Life's woes defeated and done,
The mighty dream stands tall and fair

It matters not the gnarled cage,
It matters not what people do or say,
For upon life's fretful stage
Our dreams will always save the day!

Gertrude and "Fudge"

Inseparable they would trudge,
Old Gertrude and dear Fudge,
Along grass verge and road,
Happily the world they both bestrode

Gertrude, enjoying a sunny day,
As gaily Fudge would play,
His snout in all, about and alive,
On every smell he would thrive

Old Fudge, always true to form,
Like a fur-ball caught in a wild windstorm,
His owner never happier nor more content
Than those walks with little Fudge on the scent

And on, the years did wane and go,
And their walks, in rain, sun and snow,
Then alas, Gertrude was no more,
And, her dear companion not the same as before

Came people to take little Fudge one day,
But silent and sharp had he stolen away,
They found him reposed at Gertrude's graveside,
His calm demeanour his death from a broken-heart belied

And sometimes, so very late at night,
In a faint glimmer of shimmering light,
People say, can still be seen
Old Gertrude and dear Fudge, together serene!

Saved by a Woman's Love

A sorry and abject wretch was I,
Before I drank from the fount of love,
Lonely pleas to an empty sky
Brought pure blessing from above

Came the love of a woman,
Most unselfish and sublime,
It was then that life began,
Contentment at last mine

And in her warm embrace I lay,
Her bounteous love my sweet succour,
Forever to greet the day,
With this woman I do so adore,

Her soft words a stirring melody,
Her eyes a celebration,
Life no longer a sad threnody,
My Love, My Salvation!

The Drummer Boy

From battle's fearsome fray
Marched the phalanx in martial array,
Midst the vile cacophony of war,
Man's fatal error to the fore

While soldiers courageous perished
Lost hopes and dreams cherished,
Marched a mere boy, a little frame,
Yet his hand a steady, beating refrain

The foul and fierce field a harsh bed of sharp steel,
And to shot and shell the men began to reel,
A vast swathe of shattered bone and blood
First a trickle, then a fearsome flood

Although hearts proud began to crumble,
And resolve soon began its tumble,
The little drummer boy marched ahead,
Not bowed by fear, foe nor dread

His marble eyes intense and intent,
His drum the smoke-filled air did rent,
Could be heard its pure pulse and beat,
A noble challenge to vile defeat

To the mortal men a sought sign,
His ragged redcoat almost divine,
They sallied forth tired, tense and torn ,
But not beaten, nor forlorn

And as the colours glorious flew,
And victory to these brave few,
The little drummer boy then succumbed,
His hidden wound in battle's ardour numbed

Ross Dix-Peek

To these hardened soldiers soft tears,
For this mere boy who conquered their fears,
A little Angel in a dirty redcoat,
Who won a noble victory most remote!

The Wedding Ring!

The wedding ring I wear
upon my finger,
Is far more than just that,
It is in essence a most majestic
golden-band forged on a white-hot anvil
of unconditional and eternal love
within the deepest recesses of my burning,
beating heart, a most enduring
and indestructible bond that
transcends time immortal, and
forever binds my fevered soul
to this flame-haired Goddess
of my destiny,
Sweet love and passion incarnate,
My Dearest Aphrodite…

Ross Dix-Peek

War!

The charnel stench of war,
Foul and foetid mire,
The Politicians abject whore,
Mortal man's martial desire

Tranquil peace torn asunder,
A most savage sanguine stain,
On high the Gods of Thunder,
Naught but the living dead remain

Like willing puppets they cavort,
Upon a blood-drenched stage,
Sweet sanity cut most short
In a great glare of blinding rage

Crimson Red the rivers run,
Midst a cacophony of hell,
A canvas of torn flesh under a zealous sun,
And the lonely sound of a tolling bell

Here be the Devil's playground,
Mans' dire folly to the fore,
Where vile death and madness resound,
The sad, sad threnody of War!

What is Patriotism I Ask?

What is Patriotism I ask?
And why, oh why
When called to task
Are people so willing to die?

When the martial music is still,
And the bugle and beating drum cease,
And warm blood begins to spill,
Then what of life's short lease?

And in the dark bowels of a coffin shroud
What does a mere flag mean?
When the victorious Reaper struts proud,
Death's wail shrill and obscene

And onward, onward all,
Do the great masses still plodder,
Ready to answer the clarion call,
Naught but cannon-fodder!

Ross Dix-Peek

I Grieve!

Beloved Father, Dear Sister
Gone you are,
No more,
Never again with me
to walk this mortal floor

And although the years
Be many,
I still do grieve,
My broken, shattered heart.
Knows no end nor reprieve

Often, your ethereal spectres'
Haunt my dreams,
A parade of
convulsive tears
And silent screams

So many things
Still to say;
Lost words that
Haunt my
every day!

And after all these years,
I still can't look
At the photos on the wall,
Heart still far too sore,
Sorrow still a great, dark pall!

But too, do wonderful memories
Flood my very mind,
Emotions both joyous and sad,
All at the same time!

My only comfort be,
that in Sweet Heaven above,
My Beloved Father and Dear Sister
know that I will them forever Love!

And come the day
I too do succumb,
Together we will again be,
Forever as "One"!

Ross Dix-Peek

The Actress

She stares forlorn
At her face worn,
The countenance of youth gone
Like the rays of a setting sun

Her sore heart so longs for yesterdays
When she was but the sum of her vanities,
She remembers the torrid, fevered embrace
Of an enraptured crowd, a vast adoring face

For that is sadly all she is
For without them is gone life's kiss,
She was but an unreal creation
Of man and the wiles feminine

To them but an object of desire
A mere "thing" to admire,
But now mother-time her beauty has undone
And now her most fickle flock does her shun

To the lonely floor she falls
Tears awash in great waterfalls,
Each furrow upon her face
Her beauty now does deftly deface

For vile vanity was but her stage
Her great, gilded lair and cage,
But now all she has is but regret
As mother-time and all her does forget!

(Pulchritude is but fleeting!)

The Philosophers!

Round the table sits the Cabal
Philosophers, great minds all,
And do upon the world pontificate,
To each other its woes communicate

Borne aloft are the words of these erudite
Who in their verbosity do so delight,
And serious do discuss matters Ontological,
Of Epistemology and the Metaphysical

And since time immemorial
Have so many men waxed lyrical,
Too, convinced of their great sagacity
When merely bombastic and just haughty

And naught did their abstract concepts do,
Did not feed the hungry and their abject retinue,
Naught did their pompous words achieve,
Still the piteous poor their plight solemn grieve

And what is the use of Wisdom and Intellect
If we cannot egalitarian change effect,
What is the use of a great mind and brain
If we cannot even help our fellow-man!

Ross Dix-Peek

The Politician

Beware, for I am the son of Machiavelli
The "Pretender" immortal,
From my lips pour forth only pure cunning,
My Gilded words drip with honeyed seduction

Glib-tongued and the prince of artifice
I thee will enthral,
A promise of all things I thee give
Things all

My words a golden fleece will weave
Yet only to deceive,
And when my position untenable becomes I fear not,
for just another cause I shall as quickly embrace

A vile and cunning mercenary am I,
Golden ingots my god
Unassailable Power my desire,
Naught will stand in my way

I shall seize the day!
Loyalty, I thee hate
Betrayal, I thee love

I am but a chameleon
My shameful colours changing with each passing day,
And yet, although thee know I am but a mountebank and
        charlatan,
Ye still my vile countenance and mien embrace

Ye still into my web of treachery doth stumble
Aware ye fully of my lies and duplicity
And that my dear friend,
is why I shall for all times eternal prosper!
For am I not the son of Machiavelli!

What Looks Back at Me?

My eyes heavenward fly
To rest upon a celestial sky,
And then do thoughtful ponder
As to what may lie yonder

While I upon this temporal orb stand
Just a mere speck among a sea of sand,
What is it I would beyond the stars could but see?
And what could be looking back at me?

Ah, what lies beyond this supernal curtain?
Well, no man can be certain
But could it be thee, O' Creator?
Or just another me on some planet backwater

Is there beyond this ocean of stars
A being who the same question asks?
And who also does but wonder
If the worlds beyond are indeed better

And when we both our mortal cloaks shed
And when we're both stone cold dead,
Will our lonely souls then nowhere go?
Or just midst cosmic nothingness flow?

No, I prefer to believe,
That the bright pulsing stars I do perceive
Are the welcoming eyes of my loving God,
Whose arms will be there for me when I life have shod!

Ross Dix-Peek

No Such Thing as Democracy!

People love to talk of Democracy,
But, like a dog without fleas,
Truth be told, arrant fallacy,
Merely subjugation in varying degrees,
For, no matter time nor age,
Life has never been fair,
Never without its cage,
The wolf forever in lair,
Man cares not for equality,
And sentiments noble and divine,
His only concern is his reality,
And to drink of life's sweet wine,
And thus ever will be,
The vile Fat Cat,
Wealth, caste and hierarchy,
And the poor Drowned Rat!

Sublimation 360

When we were children,
We would always let our
Emotions out,
Say what we felt,
Jump, scream and shout,

But then society deemed
that wrong, and insisted
we sublimate,
Whereupon we were
Taught to hide normal
Feelings, such as anger,
frustration, sorrow and hate

For society this was
All very good and well,
But for many folk
this meant living in
their own little Hell

And then many
Years on, when it
All became far too much,
These selfsame people
would then need to see
Psychologists and such

This they did in
Order to fully understand,
Those selfsame feelings
The world had
originally banned

So it was that many
Years, and loads
Of cash,
Were then spent to
Avoid a society-induced
Psychological "crash"

And thus can
We see life's
Vicious cycle,
Which all began by
Suppressing emotions
Most natural and vital

And what does this teach us,
Indeed, what lesson?
That's easy, to heck with Society,
Always be your own person!

Sweet Nessie!

Oh sweet Nessie, are you there?
'Neath the cold clear waters of your lair,
Or are you but legendary,
To remain but cryptozoology

Oh, great aquatic megapod
Do come out to upon the waters plod,
So we can at last put paid
To all the fuss, man-made

Was that grainy picture you?
That did great speculation brew,
Ah, that pic caused quite a stir!
But then gone again you were

And over the years people still say
That they have in truth seen you cavort and play,
So then I must ask, my dear denizen,
When will we see you again?

Or does your great bold chest
Often the still waters of Loch Ness crest,
Possibly, at that time of day
When all the folk have gone away

Whatever may be the mystery
The world sure needs you Nessie,
For no story looms larger
Than the Tale of the Loch Ness Monster!

Ross Dix-Peek

The Hunter and the Hunted

Twas the year eighteen-seventy-three
In Darkest Africa, you see,
That these events did transpire,
Events most dire

A hunter came a-hunting in the midday sun,
Montagu was his name, an Englishman,
It was but sport to him,
And the killing merely a whim

But in the bush, midst the tall elephant-grass,
Lay a lioness, too a killing machine, lean and fast,
She and her cubs just basking in the baking sun,
Not aware of what their way was to come

And gaily through the veld marched old Montagu
While behind him trudged his weary retinue,
Ah, he could not wait to his trophies show
To the folk back home and in their adulation glow

But, in the interim the lioness had seen this stranger
Who would her dear little cubs endanger,
Her fiery eyes were now intent
And her mind upon this interloper bent

But, Montagu of all of this was soundly unaware,
As he upon the majestic veld enraptured did stare,
And as the sun began to wane upon an African day
Who was now the predator and who the prey?

The end came sharp and ever so swift
As the lioness the long tall grass did rift,
And no sound did her presence announce
As she did upon Montagu pounce

No time did he have to raise his gun,
No time did he have to run,
And soon the fearful deed was over
And poor Montagu was no longer

And as his torn body in the sunburnt grass lay,
The Lioness then did most silent melt away,
And it was not long before the vultures over their meal fought,
The fresh flesh of an Englishman who thought killing mere
    sport!

Ross Dix-Peek

The Immigrant's Lament

Oh cold, cumbered foreign shore
I do thee so implore,
For warmth and respite
From this my sad, dejected plight

To these lands I did hat in hand come
Seeking a better future, sweet freedom,
Yet now so very beleaguered I do feel,
A drowning soul upon its keel

For my family I did joyous venture
To embrace this cold unhappy censure,
For them I gave my tomorrow
So that they may not my sorrow know

And each day beneath this unforgiving sky
I do the sweet heavens on high
Beseech for blessings and times fertile,
Yet still this torrid land does me so revile

For my family I do the empty streets endless trudge
Needs be but a hopeful drudge,
But oh cruel mistress I do so solemn decree
Where is thy great bounteous mercy?

Each day I know only but the lash of a foreign tongue,
Great toil and sweat I give for my dear wife and young,
And yet the faint spectre of hope is nowhere to be seen
This new day like the last, is just as obscene

And still do I these stygian depths plumb,
As I through the pages of my gilded dreams thumb,
Each day still I willingly give of my humble life
To stem my dear family's mortal strife

Oh, how I miss the warm kiss of my native land,
Again to upon its sweet, sweet soil stand,
And yet, so very deep within
I know it is upon this soil that my family's life shall begin

So, oh vile and cruel shore
Even though I thee so deplore,
Come great feast or mere crumb
Never shall I ever succumb

Come cold stinging rain
Or awful and eternal pain,
I here shall solemn and steadfast stay,
For their tomorrows, I willingly give my today!

Contact! (A War Poem)

The tracer lights up the night sky
All around bullets fly
A great cacophony of sound
"Zip", "Zing", the rounds sing,
As they bite deep into the ground

Where is the enemy?
Where could the buggers be?
Can't see a damn thing!
Mind agog, I kiss my wedding ring,
And hug mother-earth close to me

My fearful heart pounds away
Will I survive this awful day!
Great dollops of cold sweat burn my eyes
As more bullets my way flies,
And in the wet sand I lay

"Zip", "Zing", the sounds of combat ring
a great battle unfolding,
I frantically clutch my rifle
My only means of survival
And fire at every thing

"Grenade", someone bellows,
Off it goes, and in its wake death sows
Feel a mighty blow to my leg!
"don't want to die, God," I beg,
And the bright red blood flows…

I lie completely still
Hear the medic, his voice shrill
Consciousness fades in and out
"Casevac" I hear the men shout
I think of home, far beyond this lonely hill

I fall asleep, to awake but later
And far below the Devil's crater,
I smile as we ascend into the air
The door-gunner's gentle hand upon my hair,
And just another forgotten Gladiator.

Fate is but a Choice!

Fate is but a choice,
Destiny a masked virtue,
Our actions our voice,
False or most true

Even in times most dire
And events so bleak,
Life's vexed coil we sire,
Life's fleeting treasures we seek

Our naked emotions to the fore,
Great friend or foul foe,
Resonating forevermore,
Fevered joy or foetid woe,

Although Life's mortal bell
Tolls most true and deep,
It's our choices that tell,
And Destiny is but our "Keep"!

The Limited Mind

All we have is the limited mind
In itself abject failure defined,
Sheer bombast its only reprieve,
All with which to ably deceive

For man the empty word,
Turgid and so terribly absurd,
Yet taken to mean so very much,
In essence, merely the deceptive touch

Inflated tomes of illusive wind,
All with which to ably rescind
the great golden logic long forgot,
but, the stroked and vile ego man's true lot

But, what does it all mean,
Man's dear delusions so very obscene,
A dark dungeon most fevered, foetid and foul,
The petty pretence of the flawed mind's silly scowl

Planet Korgil and the Earth Marines, 2310 AD

In the Universe of the Great Blue Sun,
Which even the outer realms do shun,
Nestles the small planet, Korgil,
A place of great lore if you will

It was once an earthly colony,
With vast mineral wealth you see,
But blessed it was not, oh no,
A veritable hell as planets go

But man's greed knows no end,
And upon dark desire he does depend,
So forthwith went a small and hardy band
Of earthlings to settle that most far land

At first things went good and well,
Apart from the yellow sand and awful smell,
Inured, soldiers and settlers soon became,
And things looked fine all the same

But in the harsh barren lands to the west,
Lived vile creatures, an audacious and dangerous pest,
The Sandlings, as they were contemptuously known,
Who lived deep in the desert, windswept and blown

At first the vile ones kept far and away,
Now and again to be seen in the light of day,
But as the settlement began to encroach and expand,
There began a tussle for raw minerals and precious land

The humans at first prevailed it seemed,
But then fickle fate a different course deemed,
And in the dark recesses of a coal-black night
The Sandlings struck with primal might

Not a soul nor soldier was left alive,
Not women nor child were to survive,
But, a dying message last minute sent,
Back on earth the Supreme Council hell-bent.

No surrender nor abandonment they vowed,
These ghastly vermin would soon be cowed,
For to man greed and wealth weighs all,
For to man, mammon the compelling shawl

So back to Korgil the earthlings went,
An ad-hoc military force too hastily sent,
Primed and prepared they were ultimately not,
And yet again befell dark disaster and rank-rot

Upon earth, more panic and sheer mayhem,
But, across the celestial divide a message to them,
Miraculously, survivors there were it seems,
A small group of indomitable Earth Marines

Hold on , we're coming! was the council's call,
As the bold marines held back the unrelenting wall,
So it was that "Venture I" from the planet Krill was sent,
But, was it too late before the survivors were done and spent?

And on Korgil, and in the harsh yellow sands,
Fought the marines with cold steel and bare hands,
But most savage was the Sandlings relentless onslaught,
Foul creatures, fearful of nothing and naught

With slimy bulbous bellies, gnashing fangs and red ragged
    eyes,
Their scimitar claws reaped dire death beneath galactic skies,
And on they came, an endless and ceaseless flood,
The desolate sands a-wet and awash with mingling blood

And then, a most silent and haunting refrain
Settled snug upon the jagged bodies of the fallen and slain,
As the bloodied Sandlings silently withdrew
From the raging battlefield, now just a dwindling few

Midst the Earth Marines a stolid sanguine heap,
Not a single soldier's life sold fleeting nor cheap,
And although in waxen flesh and crimson blood reposed,
Of the teeming Alien horde they had valiantly disposed!

Then it was that Venture I and sweet providence arrived,
And among the fateful fallen found those who had survived,
And still today there can be heard excited chatter and talk
Of those brave Earth Marines who unflinching would not
  baulk

But what was it all for, that most glorious sacrifice?
Midst the pulsing heavens that do so ever entice,
Was their precious lifeblood and youth spilt in vain?
Merely for temporal want and abhorrent greedy gain!

And then, a most silent and haunting refrain
Settled snug upon the jagged bodies of the fall'n and slain.
As the bloodied Sandlings silently withdrew
From the raging battlefield, now just a dwindling few

Midst the Earth Marines a stold sanguine heap,
Not a single soldier's life sold fleeting nor cheap,
And although in waxen flesh and crimson blood exposed,
Of the teeming Alien horde they had valiantly disposed!

Then it was that Venture! and sweet providence arrived,
And among the fated, fallen found those who had survived.
And still today there can be heard excited chatter and talk
Of those brave Earth Marines who unflinching would not
    balk

But what was it all for, that most glorious sacrifice?
Midst the pulsing heavens that do so ever entice,
Was their precious lifeblood and youth spilt in vain?
Merely for temporal want and abhorrent, greedy gain!